Who Will Plant a Tree?

Written by Jerry Pallotta and Illustrated by Tom Leonard

To Abby, Hannah, and Emma, who planted a tree of joy in my head

J. P.

For my agent, Libby Ford

T. L.

Sleeping Bear Press™
2395 South Huron Parkway, Suite 200
Ann Arbor, MI 48104
www.sleepingbearpress.com

Printed and bound in the United States.

20 19 18 17 16 15 14 13 12

Library of Congress Cataloging-in-Publication Data

Pallotta, Jerry.
Who will plant a tree? / written by Jerry Pallotta ; illustrated by Tom Leonard.
p. cm
ISBN 978-1-58536-502-9
1. Trees—Seeds—Dispersal—Juvenile literature. 2. Seeds—Dispersal—Juvenile literature.
I. Leonard, Thomas, 1955- II. Title.
QK929.P35 2010
582.16—dc22   2009037411

I wonder who will plant a tree?

Last fall a squirrel buried an acorn.

He didn't know it, but he planted an oak tree!

Seeds stuck to the messy fur of an apple-eating black bear.

The bear tripped, a seed fell off, and he planted an apple tree!

A goose migrated with a chestnut burr stuck to her feathers.

Miles away, the burr came off. She planted a chestnut tree!

A dolphin pushed a coconut into ocean currents.

The coconut floated to an island and a palm tree grew!

Ants marched a pine nut down their tunnel.

They didn't know it. They planted a pine tree!

Cherry seeds got caught on the tail of a wild horse.

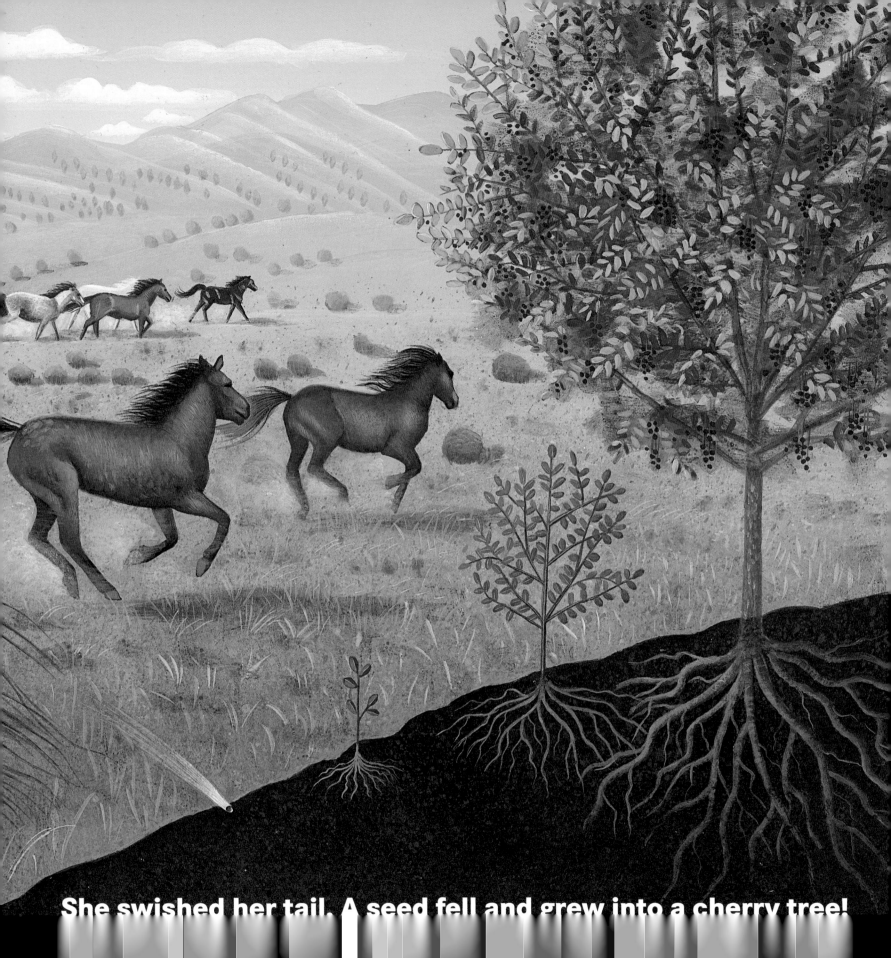

She swished her tail. A seed fell and grew into a cherry tree!

A beaver used his sharp teeth to chop down a maple tree.

Crash! Maple trees were planted along the riverbank!

Playful monkeys threw figs at each other.

They planted fig trees! Stop it! Don't throw food!

A moose got a pear tree branch stuck in its antlers.

It walked and walked. As pears fell off, trees were planted!

An owl swallowed a mouse that had been eating elm tree seeds.

Later, the owl coughed up an owl pellet and an elm tree grew!

In the Amazon River, a pacu ate floating fruit.

It pooped seeds. Trees were planted all over the rainforest!

A camel chewed some dates and then spit the seeds out.

It wasn't long before a seed grew into a date palm tree!

A wren flies to her nest with a juniper berry in her beak.

Oops! The tasty berry fell. The wren planted a juniper tree!

A teacher taught her students all about trees.

They went on a field trip and planted trees! What fun!

Wait a second! Did an elephant plant a tree?